INDOOR AND OUTDOOR GAMES

WILLIAM G. BENTLEY

Physical Education Instructor
Broward County (Florida) Schools

David S. Lake Publishers
Belmont, California

ISBN-0-8224-3910-7

Library of Congress Catalog Card Number: 66-28925

Printed in the United States of America.

PREFACE

Any teacher who has poked through the hopeless accumulation of a "game file," as the author has, in the forlorn hope that something usable will turn up, will welcome *Indoor and Outdoor Games*. This book is designed to be a handy reference for the teacher or recreation leader looking for games suitable to particular elementary grade levels.

Games are grouped together by grade level and then subdivided according to whether they are indoor or outdoor games. To increase the usefulness of the book even further, games are categorized by type—circle games, line games, etc.—in the Index. There, too, the busy teacher will find each category broken down by grade level. Thus, a teacher looking for a tag game appropriate for Grade 2, for example, need not read through a dozen games better suited to other grade levels before finding the right one.

For *Indoor and Outdoor Games*, the author has drawn on more than eleven years experience as a camp athletic counselor and as a physical education teacher in the elementary grades. Each of the almost 200 games in the book has been tested personally.

All provide useful physical development or recreation experiences. Only games that call for little or no equipment are included. Where equipment is needed, it is of a kind that might reasonably be expected to be available in schools and recreation centers.

Games may be used exactly as described, or they may be adapted by the teacher. For example, games stressing individual effort may be adapted as team games. The reverse is also possible. And of course, the children themselves will find many new ways to play these games.

As with all recreation and athletic activities, excitement and high spirits can lead to mishaps. Suggestions that could help prevent accidents are given when applicable. With even a minimum of supervision, however, the games in this book are as safe to play as they are fun to play. And fun they are. Try them and see!

WILLIAM G. BENTLEY

CONTENTS

GRADES K-2

INDOOR GAMES

BIRD, BEAST, FISH

Equipment: None. A player chosen to be *It* stands in front of the class. He calls out a player's name and then says "Bird, beast, fish . . . beast." Then he starts counting to ten. Before he finishes the count, the player whose name he called must name a beast that has not been named previously. If he can do this before *It* can count to ten, he becomes the new *It*. If he fails to do so, *It* calls on another player to name a bird, beast, or fish in the same manner.

BUMBLEBEE AND BUTTERFLIES

Equipment: None. A player selected to be *The Bumblebee* hides in the room. A player chosen to be *The Mother Butterfly* taps seven other *Butterflies* and they follow her about the room. When the leader calls "Look for *The Bumblebee*," the *Butterflies* walk quickly

1

back to their seats. As he tries to tag them, *The Bumblebee* hums and buzzes. The last *Butterfly* tagged chooses the next *Bumblebee* and *Mother Butterfly.*

BUTTON, BUTTON

Equipment: A button. The players stand facing in a circle. A player chosen to be *It* stands in the middle of the circle with his eyes closed and counts aloud to fifteen. While he is doing this, the rest of the players pass the button around the circle. They stop when *It* reaches fifteen. *It* opens his eyes and is allowed three guesses as to who has the button. If he guesses correctly, he changes places with the one who has the button.

CALL NAME TAG

Equipment: None. A player chosen to be *It* stands in front of the room. The leader calls the names of two players who must change places. While they change places, either one may be tagged by *It.* If one is tagged, he becomes *It* for the next game. For variety, players may be told to walk, hop, skip, etc., while changing places.

DOG AND BONE

Equipment: Chalkboard eraser or beanbag. A player chosen to be *The Dog* sits in a chair in front of the classroom with his back to the other players. *The Bone* (the eraser) is on the floor under his chair. The leader points to a player. This player quietly leaves his desk and walks up and tries to grab *The Bone.* If *The Dog* hears him coming, he says "Arf, arf," and the player must return to his seat. If *The Dog* does not hear him and he succeeds in getting *The Bone,* he becomes the new *Dog.*

HESITATION

Equipment: None. The players stand to the right side of their seats. Alternate rows face the back of the room. When a signal to start is given (or when music is played), everyone starts to follow a designated leader. They follow him about the room, down one aisle then up another, until the signal to stop is given (or the music stops). Then all players must stop where they are and remain motionless. Anyone who moves is eliminated and has to take his seat. The last player remaining becomes the new leader.

HUCKLE, BUCKLE, BEANSTALK

Equipment: A small object—key, chalk, etc. A player selected to be leader hides a small object while the other players keep their eyes closed. When the leader says "Ready," the players start looking around the room for the hidden item. When a player sees the object, he goes to the leader and says "Huckle, buckle, beanstalk." Then he sits down in his seat. After five players inform the leader that they have seen the object, a new game is started. The first player to locate the object becomes the new leader.

HUNTSMAN

Equipment: None. The players are seated in rows. A chosen leader wanders up and down the aisles and asks "Who would like to go with me and hunt ducks (or bears, lions, etc.)?" As the leader passes, the players who wish to go with him follow him in single file. Glancing back now and then, the leader waits until the players are a good distance from their seats. Then he turns and shouts "Bang." At this, all the players walk to their seats. The first one to reach his seat becomes the new leader.

IT IS I

Equipment: None. A player selected to be *It* comes to the front of the room and turns his back to the class. The leader motions another player to come up and knock on the floor behind *It*. *It* asks "Who is there?" The player who did the knocking, trying to disguise his voice, says "It is I." Then he returns to his place. When the leader says "Ready," *It* turns around and is permitted two guesses as to who did the knocking. If correct, he continues to be *It*. If not, the person who knocked becomes *It*.

JACK BE NIMBLE

Equipment: Milk carton. The players line up in front of the candle-stick (milk carton) and take turns trying to jump over it. As they jump, they say:

Jack, be nimble.
Jack, be quick.
Jack, jump over the candlestick.

Those who are unsuccessful are eliminated from the game.

KEEP A SECRET

Equipment: Thimble or chalk. This game is played by rows. The players in the row selected by the leader to start the game put their heads down while the leader hides the thimble. When told to look up, they go around the room searching. When a player spots the object, he returns to his seat without revealing the location of the object. The last one to be seated is the loser. Anyone giving away the secret goes out of the game.

LOST CHILD

Equipment: None. A player chosen to be *It* goes to the front of the room, closes his eyes, and turns his back to the class. The leader then signals all the other players to change seats. While this is going on, the leader selects one player to hide outside the classroom. Then *It* is told to turn around and is given three chances to name the player missing from the room. If he guesses correctly, he can be *It* again. If he does not, the leader chooses another player to be *It*.

MAGIC CARPET

Equipment: Squares of construction paper. Paper squares are placed on the floor, one for each player. The players skip around the squares. At a signal from the leader, they try to stand on one of the squares. While they have been skipping, the leader has removed one of the squares, so one player will not be able to find a square and must leave the game. After each stop, a square is removed. The game goes on until only one player is left. Music can be used to start and stop movement.

OBJECT TOUCHING

Equipment: None. The first player selected by the leader leaves his seat, touches an object, and returns to his seat. The second player touches the same object, plus another one. Player number three repeats the process and adds another object. When a player cannot remember all the objects he must touch, the game is over and the leader selects a player to start the next game.

RAILROAD TRAIN

Equipment: None. Each player is named for some part of a train—engine, mail car, wheels, whistle, etc. A player chosen to be *The Trainmaster* tells a story using the names of the parts of a train. As each part of a train is mentioned, the player with that name takes his place in line and puts his hands on the shoulders of the one ahead of him. When the train is complete, *The Trainmaster* gives the signal for the train to move ahead.

SALMON AND BEARS

Equipment: None. This game is played by one row at a time. A player in a row is chosen to be *The Bear*. The rest of the players in the row are *The Salmon*. *The Bear* hides behind or under the leader's desk (*The Log*), and *The Salmon* "swim" up to *The Log*. One of *The Salmon* hits the desk with his "fin," and that is the signal for *The Bear* to go after *The Salmon*. He tries to tag as many as possible before they get back to their seats (*Deep Pool*). The game continues until every row has had a turn.

SQUIRREL AND NUT

Equipment: Thimble or chalk. A player chosen to be *The Squirrel* hides *The Nut* (thimble) in his hands. The other players sit with their heads down, eyes closed, and one hand cupped in front of them. *The Squirrel* moves quietly about the room and drops *The Nut* into one of the cupped hands. That player gets up and chases *The Squirrel* back to his seat (*Nest*). If *The Squirrel* reaches his *Nest*, he is safe and goes around once again. If he is tagged, the player who tags him becomes the new *Squirrel*.

TRAVELING HOME

Equipment: None. The leader chooses a player and starts the game by saying "Go by boat to Linda's house." The player must imitate a boat trip. When he arrives at "Linda's house," he tells her to "Go to Jimmy's house by bicycle." The game continues until everyone has taken a trip. Trips can be made in a variety of ways —skip, hop, gallop, etc.

WEATHER BUREAU

Equipment: None. A player chosen to be *The Weather Bureau* calls out which way the wind is blowing. All the other players must face in the direction *The Weather Bureau* says the wind is blowing. Players who face in the wrong direction are out of the game. If "tornado" is called, the players must pivot around several times. After the game has gone on a short time, a new *Weather Bureau* is chosen.

WHO HAS LEFT THE RING?

Equipment: None. The players form a circle around a player chosen to be *It*. *It* must keep his eyes closed. Another player is then selected and he stands behind one of the other players in the circle. *It* is then permitted to open his eyes. He is allowed one guess as to who has left the ring. If *It* guesses correctly, the player who left the ring becomes the new *It*.

OUTDOOR GAMES

ANIMAL

Equipment: None. A player chosen to be *It* stands in front of the other players and imitates an animal. When somebody correctly guesses the animal imitated, he chases *It* to a designated goal. If *It* reaches the goal without being tagged, he is still *It*. If he gets tagged, the player who tags him becomes *It*.

BEANBAG PILE

Equipment: One beanbag for each team. The players are divided into four equal teams lined up in single-file formations, players in a line an arm's length apart. At the leader's signal, the first player in each squad runs to a designated line fifty feet away, lays his beanbag on that line, and returns and tags the next player on his team. The second player then runs to the line, picks up the beanbag, and runs back and hands it to the third player, etc. The team that finishes first wins. For variety, tell the runners to skip, hop, etc. This is a good activity to stress the proper way to tag. The returning runner should tag the next runner's right hand with his right hand. This avoids the danger of having players running into each other.

BEAR IN THE PIT

Equipment: None. The players stand facing in a circle holding hands. A player chosen to be *The Bear* stands in the middle of the circle. At a signal, he crawls out of the circle. The two players holding hands at the spot where *The Bear* gets out must chase him and tag him. The first one to tag him is the new *Bear*.

BOUNCE THE BALL

Equipment: Utility ball. The players stand three feet apart facing in a circle. A leader is selected to go to the middle of the circle. He bounces the ball to someone in the circle. If that player does not catch it, he is out of the game and must kneel down. The last one standing wins the game. The game may then be continued from the kneeling position. In this version, all the players who miss must sit down.

BROWNIES AND ELVES

Equipment: None. Two equal teams, *The Brownies* and *The Elves*, stand at goal lines about twenty-five yards apart. *The Elves* stand with their backs to *The Brownies*. Silently, *The Brownies* creep up on *The Elves* and stand behind them. Then the leader of *The Brownies* calls out "Run, *Brownies*, run!" *The Brownies* hurry back towards their own goal line and *The Elves* turn around and pursue them. Any *Brownies* tagged must go over to the other team. Then it is *The Brownies'* turn. They turn their backs and *The Elves* creep up on them. The team having the most players at the end of the playing time is the winner.

BUSY BEE

Equipment: None. Each player has a partner except a player chosen to be *It.* The couples scatter and the leader calls out various commands, such as "Back to back," "Face each other," and "Shake hands." When the leader calls out "Busy bee," everyone has to get a new partner, including *It.* The player who fails to secure a new partner is the new *It.*

CAT AND RAT

Equipment: None. One player is chosen to be *The Cat* and another *The Rat.* The rest of the players hold hands in a circle. *The Cat* stands outside of the circle and *The Rat* stands inside. *The Rat* says "I am *The Rat,*" and *The Cat* replies "I am *The Cat.*" *The Rat* says "You can't catch me," and *The Cat* says "Oh yes I can." Then *The Cat* starts chasing *The Rat* in and out of the circle. The players in the circle help *The Rat* by letting him in and out, but they try to keep *The Cat* from catching *The Rat* by raising and lowering their hands. If *The Cat* does not catch *The Rat* after a reasonable length of time, a new *Cat* and a new *Rat* are chosen.

CHARLIE OVER THE WATER

Equipment: None. A player is chosen to be *Charlie.* All the other players then join hands in a circle and walk or skip to the right. As they go around they chant:

> Charlie over the water,
> Charlie over the sea,
> Charlie caught a bluebird,
> But he can't catch me.

When the players complete the chant, they all stoop low. *Charlie* tries to tag one of them before he can stoop. If he does, that player becomes *Charlie.*

CIRCLE CALL BALL

Equipment: Utility ball. All the players except one form a large circle. Each player is given a number. The extra player stands in the middle of the circle and starts the game by tossing the ball up in the air and calling out a number. The player with the number called must run and try to catch the ball on the fly or on the first bounce. This player then tosses the ball up and calls out another number. One point is scored for a ball caught on the first bounce and two points for a ball caught on the fly. This game can also be used without scoring, as a skill activity.

CIRCLE TOSS BALL

Equipment: Playground ball. The players stand in a large circle. The leader stands in the middle of the circle and tosses the playground ball to each player. If the ball is caught and tossed correctly, the player may sit or stoop down. If either the catch or the toss is incorrect, the player remains standing and waits for another turn. This is definitely a skill game and should be used for this purpose. It can also be used as a race between two circles to see which circle can be seated first.

COCONUTS IN MAY

Equipment: None. Two teams of players line up facing each other on goal lines about twenty feet apart. One team walks up to the other and says:

> Here we go gathering coconuts in May,
> Coconuts in May, coconuts in May,
> Here we go gathering coconuts in May,
> So early in the morning.

The first team calls out the name of a player on the second team. The person named comes to the middle to engage in a tug of war with one of the players on the first team. A point is scored for the team whose player pulls the other player over its goal line.

DROP THE HANDKERCHIEF

Equipment: A handkerchief. The players stand facing in a circle. A player chosen to be *It* runs around the outside of the circle and drops the handkerchief behind one of the players in the circle. When this player sees the handkerchief behind him, he picks it up and chases *It*. If *It* gets back to the empty place in the circle before the player chasing him can tag him, the chaser then becomes *It*. If *It* gets tagged by the player chasing him, he is still *It*.

DUCK, DUCK, GOOSE

Equipment: None. A player is selected to be *It*. All the other players stoop in a circle. *It* walks around the outside of the circle and touches each player lightly on the head, repeating the words "duck, duck, duck." When *It* taps a player and says "duck, duck, goose," that player jumps up and chases him. If the player tags *It*, *It* goes to the center of the circle and the player becomes the new *It*. If the player fails to tag *It*, he returns to his place in the circle and *It* goes around the circle again.

EXCHANGE TAG

Equipment: None. A player is chosen to be *It*. The other players form two equal teams and face each other about thirty feet apart. The leader calls out the names of two players, one from each team. These players try to trade places before *It* can tag them. If a player is tagged, he becomes the new *It*. If *It* fails to tag either of them, two new names are called and the game goes on.

FIRE ENGINE

Equipment: None. A player is designated *The Fire Chief*. The other players are divided into four teams, *Fire Engines 1, 2, 3,* and *4. The Fire Chief* calls out "There is a fire at—(a tree, a bush, etc.) *Fire Engine 3* put out the blaze!" All the firemen of the fire engine named run to the designated spot and wait there until *The Fire Chief* calls out "All clear." When this signal is given, all the firemen of the fire engine named run back to their station. The first one back is the new *Fire Chief*. As a surprise, a general alarm can be given and all the fire engines are sent out.

FLOWER GARDEN

Equipment: None. The players sit or stand facing in a circle. Each is given the name of a different flower. A player is chosen to go to the middle of the circle. He says, "I enter the flower garden and want a rose and a lilac." The players with these names must then change places with each other. While they are changing places, the player in the middle tries to get a vacant place. The player left without a place must then go to the middle of the circle and repeat the process.

FLYING DUTCHMAN

Equipment: None. The players hold hands in a circle. Two players are selected to be partners. They join hands and run around the circle. The partner closest to the circle touches the joined hands of two other players. These two run around the circle in the opposite direction and try to get back to the vacant place in the circle before the first pair. Runners pass to each other's right as they go around the circle.

FOLLOW THE LEADER

Equipment: None. The players line up behind a player chosen to be leader. The leader waves his arms, runs, hops, skips, or makes any other movements he wishes. The others must do the same thing. After a reasonable length of time, a new leader is selected.

FORTY WAYS TO GET THERE

Equipment: None. All the players line up on one side of the playing area. Forty feet from the players and parallel to them, a goal line is drawn. The first player in the row is asked by the leader to cross over to this goal line in any manner he chooses. The second person then follows, etc. Each player must cross over in a different manner than those before him. If he repeats what another has done, he must return and cross over again. The player crossing over in the most original manner is the winner and becomes the leader for the next game.

FOX AND CHICKENS

Equipment: None. One player is chosen to be *The Fox* and another is chosen to be *The Mother Hen.* The rest of the players are *Chickens.* *The Chickens* line up behind *The Mother Hen.* *The Fox* tries to tag the last *Chicken* in line, but *The Mother Hen* and her line of

Chickens try to protect the last *Chicken* by turning and dodging. When the last *Chicken* is tagged, *The Fox* goes to the end of the line, the first *Chicken* becomes *The Mother Hen,* and *The Mother Hen* becomes *The Fox.*

FREEZE

Equipment: None. Players scatter over the playing area. As directed by the leader, they either skip, run, or walk. When the leader calls out "Freeze," all must remain frozen until the leader calls "Melt." Anyone moving after "Freeze" is called is eliminated from the game. Music can be substituted for calls. When the music is playing, everyone is in motion. When the music stops, everyone freezes. The last player remaining in the game becomes the leader.

FROG IN THE SEA

Equipment: None. Several players are chosen to be *Frogs.* The rest of the players kneel in a circle to form *The Sea. The Frogs* hop about inside the circle chanting "Frog in the sea, can't catch me." The players on the circle reach in and try to touch a *Frog.* If they do, they exchange places. Anyone who "falls into *The Sea*" must leave the game to "dry off."

GALLOP TAG

Equipment: None. The players form a circle. A player is chosen to be *It. It* gallops around the outside of the circle and tags a player in the circle. The player tagged must gallop around the outside of the circle after *It.* If he tags *It, It* must go to the vacant place in the circle. If *It* is not tagged after two gallops around the circle, he continues to be *It.*

GARDEN SCAMP

Equipment: None. The players hold hands in a large circle. One player is chosen to be *The Scamp;* he stands inside the circle. Another player is chosen to be *The Gardner;* he walks around the outside of the circle. When *The Gardner* sees *The Scamp,* he asks "Who let you in my garden?" *The Scamp* replies "No one" and

runs between and around the other players. While *The Scamp*
runs, he may stop and make funny movements. *The Gardner*, who
chases after *The Scamp* must stop and make the same movements.
If *The Gardner* tags *The Scamp*, *The Scamp* becomes *The Gardner*
and a new *Scamp* is chosen.

GERM AND THE TOOTHBRUSH

Equipment: None. The players (*The Teeth*) line up in a semicircle
representing *The Jaw*. One player is chosen to be *The Germ;* he
hides behind one of the players (a *Tooth*). A player is chosen to be
The Toothbrush; he stands in the middle of *The Jaw* with his eyes
closed. The teacher, or a child chosen to be leader, pretends to
cover *The Toothbrush* with toothpaste and then tells him to open
his eyes and look for *The Germ*. When *The Toothbrush* locates *The
Germ*, he chases him between and around *The Teeth* until he tags
him or the teacher stops the game and chooses a new *Germ* and a
new *Toothbrush.*

GIANT AND GNOMES

Equipment: None. The players form a large circle of *Gnomes* between two goal lines located about forty-five feet apart. A player
chosen to be *The Giant* kneels in the middle of the circle. *The
Gnomes* begin to tease him by stepping in and out of his land.
Suddenly, *The Giant* jumps up and chases *The Gnomes* to either goal
line he chooses. Anyone tagged by *The Giant* must help him in the
middle of the circle when it reforms. The last one to evade being
tagged becomes the new *Giant.*

GOOD MORNING

Equipment: None. The players stand in a circle formation. A player
chosen to be *It* runs around the outside of the circle. *It* tags a
player and keeps on running. The player tagged runs around the
circle in the opposite direction from *It*. When they meet, they both
shake hands, say "good morning," and continue running. The first
one to reach the vacant place is *It* for the next round. A player
cannot be *It* more than twice in a row.

GUESS WHO

Equipment: Utility ball. The players line up about twenty feet from a player chosen to be *It*. *It* turns his back, and the ball is passed along the line of players. At a signal from a chosen leader, the player who is holding the ball throws the ball at *It* and tries to hit him below the waist. If the player who throws the ball misses, he has to change places with *It*. If *It* is hit by the ball, he turns around and gets one guess as to who hit him. If *It* guesses correctly, he changes places with the player who threw the ball.

HAVE YOU SEEN MY FRIEND?

Equipment: None. The players are arranged in a large circle. A player is selected to be *The Tagger*. He goes around the outside of the circle. Suddenly, he tags someone in the circle and asks "Have you seen my friend?" The player tagged asks "How is your friend dressed?" *The Tagger* then describes the clothing and appearance of his friend. If the tagged player correctly guesses who the friend is, *The Tagger* steps aside. The tagged player chases the friend, who tries to reach the vacant space in the circle. If the friend is tagged before he can get to the vacant place, he then becomes the new *Tagger*. If he does not get tagged, the tagged player becomes the new *Tagger*.

HILL DILL

Equipment: None. A player chosen to be *It* stands in the middle of the playing area. The other players line up at one end of the playing area. When *It* calls out "Hill Dill, come over the hill," they try to get to the opposite end (which should be about fifty feet away). If tagged by *It*, a player must stay in the middle with *It* and help him tag the others when they cross over at the next call. It is best to mark off an area in the middle of the playing space as the territory where tags can be made.

I SAW

Equipment: None. The players form a circle. One player is chosen to go to the middle of the circle and imitate what he saw on the way to school. The players in the circle then imitate his actions.

After each of the imitations, a new player is chosen to go to the middle of the circle.

JUMP THE BROOK

Equipment: None. A space several feet wide is marked off and called *The Brook.* The players run and try to jump over it. If successful, they wait for a turn to try again. If they "get their feet wet," they are out of the game and must retire to the side. When all have had one try, make *The Brook* wider.

KEEN EYES

Equipment: None. Two equal teams stand facing each other several yards apart. One team is *It,* and its members carefully observe the appearance of the players opposite them. They note the way they are dressed, the way their hair is combed, etc. At a signal from the leader, the *It* team members turn their backs. Then each member of the other team changes something about his appearance— changes the part in his hair, unties a shoelace, etc. When the leader signals the *It* team to turn around, each of its members, in turn, tries to find out what change the player opposite him has made. He has thirty seconds in which to decide. If he names the change correctly, he scores a point for his team. The teams then change positions.

KICK OUT

Equipment: Soccer ball. Forming a circle, the players stand in stride position, foot to foot. A player selected to be *It* tries to kick the soccer ball out of the circle. The other players in the circle try to block the ball without using their hands. If the ball goes out between a player's feet, or on his right side, it is a point against him. The ball may be kicked only with the side of the foot and at a height below the waist.

LINE AND CIRCLE STAND

Equipment: None. This game is played on a blacktop area that has lines and circles. The players scatter over the blacktop area. When the leader calls "Circle," they must try to stand on part of a circle before the leader can count to five. When the leader calls "Lines," they must try to stand on part of a line before the leader can count to five. Anyone failing to reach a line or circle before the leader counts to five is eliminated.

MIDNIGHT

Equipment: None. A player chosen to be *The Fox* stands at one end of the playing area (*The Den*). A player chosen to be *The Mother Hen* lines up with her *Chicks*—the rest of the players—at the other end of the playing area. *The Mother Hen* brings her *Chicks* up to *The Fox* and asks: "Mr. Fox, what time is it?" If *The Fox* answers with any hour but midnight, *The Chicks* scamper about. *The Mother Hen* asks again. If *The Fox* says "Midnight" this time, all *The Chicks* run back to *The Chicken Yard* to escape *The Fox*. Anyone tagged by *The Fox* must help him to catch the others. The game continues until all *The Chicks* are caught.

MOTHER, MAY I?

Equipment: None. Two lines are drawn about forty feet apart. A player chosen to be *It* stands on one line; the rest of the players stand on the other line. *It* says to the first player on the line: "Take one giant step (baby step, etc.)." The player must reply "Mother, may I?" If *It* answers "Yes," the player may take the step. If *It* answers "No," the player must remain in his place. A player failing to say "Mother, may I" must go back to the starting line. The first player to reach the goal line is the new *It*.

MOUSETRAP

Equipment: None. The players stand in two circles, one inside the other. The players in the inner circle hold hands; they are *The Mousetrap*. The players in the outer circle are *The Mice;* they stand at some distance from *The Mousetrap* and do not hold hands. At a signal, the two circles start moving in opposite directions until the teacher or another leader calls "Stop." At this command, *The Mousetrap* players lift their hands and *The Mice* march in and around and out of *The Mousetrap*. Suddenly, the leader says "Trap," and *The Mousetrap* players drop their hands and try to catch *The Mice*. Those caught become part of *The Mousetrap*. The game goes on until all *The Mice* are caught.

ONE LEG TAG

Equipment: None. A player is selected to be *It*, and the other players scatter over the playing area. At a signal from the leader, *It* chases one of the other players. For a player to be safe, all he has to do is stand on one leg. If *It* tags a player while the player has both feet on the ground, that player becomes the new *It*.

PARTNER SKIP

Equipment: None. The players stand facing out in a circle, with one hand held forward. A player is then chosen to skip around the circle and touch another player's hand. These two then skip together until they come to the spot vacated by the second player. The first player remains there. The second player then skips around and touches a third player's hand. Then they skip until they come to the place vacated by the third player. The game continues until all have had a turn to skip the circle.

POSTURE WALK

Equipment: One chalkboard eraser or beanbag for each team. Five equal teams are arranged in single-file formations facing in the same direction. At a signal from the leader, the first player on each team picks up an eraser, places it on his head, and walks to a designated goal line thirty feet away. Then he goes to the end of his team's line. The player finishing first scores a point for his team. A player can not hold the eraser. If it starts to fall, he must let it hit the ground and then pick it up and place it back on his head to continue the race. This activity may also be used as a relay race. The team that completes the race before the other team is the winner.

RUN FOR YOUR SUPPER

Equipment: None. The players form a circle. A player chosen to be *It* goes around the outside of the circle. He stops between two players and puts one hand on one player's shoulder and the other hand on the other player's shoulder, saying "Run for your supper." The two players he has touched run around the circle; the one on *It's* left goes left, and the other goes right. The runner who gets back to his original place first wins and trades places with *It*. Variations can include "skip," "hop," or "walk."

RUN, RABBIT, RUN

Equipment: None. The players are divided into two teams, *The Rabbits* and *The Foxes*. *The Foxes* are scattered over the playing area. *The Rabbits*, all holding hands, walk across the playing area. When one of *The Foxes* calls out "Run, *Rabbit*, run," all *The Rabbits* run for the opposite end of the playing area. All those tagged become *Foxes*.

SCAT

Equipment: None. The players form a line facing the leader. The leader leads them in an exercise. Unexpectedly, the leader calls out "Scat." Then all try to get past the leader to a designated goal line. All those tagged by the leader have to help him the next time. The last one to be tagged becomes the leader for the next game.

SHUFFLE RELAY

Equipment: Various small objects, such as chalkboard erasers, bean-bags, etc. The players are divided into two teams lined up in single-file formations facing in the same direction. In front of each group, about forty feet away, two small circles are drawn. In the first of each of these circles, place three small objects. At a signal from the leader, the first player on each team runs to his team's circle containing the objects and with one hand moves the objects, one at a time, to his team's second circle. Then he runs back and tags the outstretched hand of the next player on his team, who repeats the process of moving the objects from one circle to the other. The team whose last player crosses the starting line first is the winner.

SIR KNIGHT

Equipment: None. Two lines are designated at each end of the playing area. One is *The Village* and the other is *The Castle*. A player is selected to be *Sir Knight* and two other players are chosen as *Guards*. The idea is for the two *Guards* to keep *Sir Knight* from being tagged by the other players on his way from *The Castle* to *The Village*. Anyone tagged by the guards has to go to *The Prison*, which is located to the side of the playing area. Whoever tags *Sir Knight* becomes the new *Sir Knight*, and he is allowed to choose two new *Guards*.

SOUP BOWL

Equipment: Bases (or chalk circles). The players stand on designated bases in a circle formation. A player selected to be *It* stands in the middle of the circle (*The Soup Bowl*). When *It* calls "Change," all the players change positions. *It* tries to secure a base during the change. If he succeeds, the player left out must go to the middle of the circle and be *It*. Any player who has been *It* twice must perform a stunt to stay in the game.

SPEEDY SQUIRREL

Equipment: None. The players stand facing in a circle. One of the players is chosen to be *Chief Squirrel*. He walks around the circle and tags five different players. They remain in their places until he calls out "Speedy squirrel." Then the five who were tagged race around the outside of the circle and try to get back to their original places. The first player to return to his place in the circle is the winner and becomes *Chief Squirrel*.

SPIDER AND FLIES

Equipment: None. Two goal lines are designated at opposite ends of a playing area. A circle is located equidistant from the two goal lines. A player called *The Spider* sits in the center of the circle while the other players, *The Flies*, walk around the circle. When *The Spider* jumps up and chases after *The Flies*, they flee towards either goal line. *The Flies* tagged become *The Spider's* helpers.

STOP AND GO

Equipment: None. The players stand in a circle formation. A player chosen to be the leader stands in the middle of the circle. When he

says "Go," he starts an active movement, such as jumping or
skipping. When he says "Stop," all must stop. If the leader stops
without saying "Stop," however, the players who stop are out.

STOP AND START

Equipment: None. The players face in the direction indicated by a
leader. At a signal to either walk, run, or skip, they start going in
that direction. When the leader blows a whistle or says "Stop,"
they all stop at once. The leader then points in another direction
and calls out "Run," "Walk," "Skip," etc. Players who do not
follow directions, or who fail to stop when the leader tells them,
are assigned to a second group that follows behind the first group.
The object of the game is to be the last player left in the first group.

STOP AND STOOP

Equipment: None. The players walk around. At the leader's command, all skip, run, gallop, etc. When the leader says "Stoop,"
they must all stoop. The last one to stoop is eliminated. The game
continues until a winner is chosen—the last player in the game. To
create more opportunity for activity, divide the players into several
teams and have a winner for each one.

STRIDE BALL

Equipment: Utility ball. The players form a circle with their legs
spread in stride position. They try to roll the ball out of the circle
between the legs of the other players. If a player succeeds in getting
the ball out of the circle, he leaves the game. The game goes on
until only a few players are left.

TEACHER AND CLASS

Equipment: A utility ball for each team. This game is played to its
best advantage if the players are divided into small teams. A
Teacher is selected for each team. The other players on each team
(*The Class*) form a semicircle about twelve feet away from their
Teacher. The Teacher tosses the ball to each player, and each player
returns the ball to *The Teacher.* When a player misses a throw

from his *Teacher*, he goes to the end of the line. If a *Teacher* misses, he becomes part of *The Class* and goes to the end of the line; the player at the front of the line becomes the new *Teacher*. The distance between each *Teacher* and his *Class* may vary according to the abilities of the players.

TELEPHONE TAG

Equipment: None. The players join hands in a circle. A player is chosen to be *The Operator;* he stands in the middle of the circle. The players forming the circle are numbered consecutively from one to nine. Then they scatter and reform in another circle with a mixed-up number sequence. *The Operator* then calls a number. Anyone with that number runs around the outside of the circle and tries to be the first one back to his vacant place.

TOMMY TINKER'S GROUND

Equipment: Pieces of yellow and white paper. A player is selected to be *Tommy Tinker*. A line is drawn to designate the boundary line of *Tommy Tinker's Ground*. Pieces of yellow and white paper, representing gold and silver, are scattered behind the boundary line. To start the game, the other players stand along the boundary line and chant:

> I'm on Tommy Tinker's ground
> Picking up gold and silver!

When they reach the word "silver," they dart across the boundary line and try to pick up as much gold and silver as they can without being tagged by *Tommy Tinker*. If tagged, they have to drop their gold and silver and go to *Tommy Tinker's Dungeon* on the side line. The player who picks up the most gold and silver without getting tagged becomes the next *Tommy Tinker*.

TRADES

Equipment: None. Two equal teams line up behind goal lines a short distance apart. The leader tells one of the teams to walk over to the other team's goal line, where the following dialogue takes place:

Team 1	*Team 2*
"Here we come."	"Where from?"
"New Orleans."	"What's your trade?"
"Lemonade."	"Show us some."

The first team then acts out some activity. When the second team guesses the activity correctly, it gives chase and tries to catch as many of the first team's members as possible. All those tagged become members of the second team. Fast walking may be substituted for running.

WATER SPRITE

Equipment: None. Players stand in two lines facing each other across a large open space called *The River.* A player chosen to be *The Water Sprite* stands in the middle of *The River* and asks a player to cross. This player then asks a player standing on the opposite "bank" to cross over. The two players attempt to trade places, and *The Water Sprite* tries to tag one of them as they cross *The River.* If he succeeds, he changes places with the player tagged.

WIND AND FLOWERS

Equipment: None. The players are divided into two equal teams, *The Wind* and *The Flowers.* The teams assemble at goal lines about twenty-five yards apart. *The Flowers* choose the name of a flower and go over and stand in front of *The Wind. The Wind* players try, in turn, to guess the name of the flower. When they guess correctly, they chase *The Flowers* back to *The Flowers'* goal line. Any *Flower* tagged becomes a member of the other team. Later, the teams exchange names, and the new *Flowers* have to think up a name for the new *Wind* to guess. The first several times this game is played, it would be advisable to have the players walk fast instead of run. Stress running in a straight line to avoid collisions.

2

GRADES 3-4

INDOOR GAMES

AUTOMOBILE RACE

Equipment: None. Each row of players chooses the name of an automobile. At the leader's signal, the first player in each alternate row leaves his seat and walks to his right around his row until he returns to his original seat. As soon as he is seated, the second player repeats the procedure. The game goes on until the last player in one of the rows returns to his seat. The row whose last player is reseated first wins. Warn the seated players to keep their feet out of the aisles.

BANDIT

Equipment: None. The players sit in a circle. When the leader points to a player in the circle and calls out "Bandit," that player must place both of his hands over his ears immediately. At the same time, each of his two neighbors must place the hand nearest *The Bandit* over his own ear on that side. The last of the three to cover his ears is out of the game and has to stand. *The Bandit* then points and calls the next "Bandit," and the game goes on. Other calls may be substituted for "Bandit."

BEASTS AND HUNTERS

Equipment: None. Eight players are selected to be *The Beasts.* They stand in the front of the room. Each chooses the name of an animal. The rest of the players are *The Hunters. The Hunters* put their heads down while *The Beasts* change the order in which they are standing. When the leader says "Awaken, *Hunters,*" all of *The Hunters* put their heads up. The leader asks certain ones to correctly name *The Beasts* in their new order. The first *Hunter* to name them correctly goes to the front of the room and chooses a new group to be *Beasts* for the next game.

CHASE THE ANIMAL

Equipment: Three chalkboard erasers or beanbags. The players form a circle. One of the erasers is given the name of an animal and started around the circle. After it goes around once, the leader starts another "animal" around the circle. This "animal" tries to catch up with the first one. After another time around, a third animal is started on its way. There is no scoring in this game.

DETECTIVE

Equipment: A small piece of chalk. A player chosen to be *The Detective* leaves the room. A piece of chalk is placed out in the open somewhere in the room. *The Detective* is then called back into the room. He wanders around looking for the piece of chalk. When he is close to it, the rest of the players clap their hands loudly. When he goes away from it, they clap softly. If *The Detective* finds the chalk, he chooses a new *Detective.* If the clapping is too noisy, the manner of hinting to *The Detective* may be changed to humming or raising and lowering hands.

ERASER RELAY

Equipment: Two chalkboard erasers. A player chosen to be *It* goes to the chalkboard and writes down the name of another player. Then he places an eraser on his head. The player whose name is written on the chalkboard comes up and erases his name, places an eraser on his head, and starts to chase *It*. If successful in tagging *It*, he becomes the new *It*. To keep the rest of the players alert, either of the runners may place his eraser on the head of anyone else in the room.

FISH NET SCRAMBLE

Equipment: None. All of the players except one are seated. The player who is standing gives each of the others the name of a fish. To start the game, he calls out the names of two different fish. The players representing these fish must exchange seats. The caller also tries to secure a seat. The player left without a seat becomes the new caller. When "Fish net scramble" is called, everyone must change seats.

GUESS WHAT I SEE

Equipment: None. The leader stands in the front of the room and selects an object somewhere in the room—one that will be difficult for the others to guess. He asks: "Guess what I see." Then he calls on players who raise their hands to guess. The first player to guess correctly becomes the next leader. Hints, such as the first letter of the object, its color, its location, etc., may be given after several players have guessed incorrectly.

I WROTE A LETTER

Equipment: None. A player selected to be *The Chalkboard* turns his back to the other players and closes his eyes. The leader then "draws" several circles on *The Chalkboard's* back. As he moves his fingers, he says: "I wrote a letter and signed it with a dot." Then he chooses someone to come up and put the dot on *The Chalkboard's* back. When this has been done, *The Chalkboard* turns around and has three guesses to find out who "signed" the dot. If successful, he remains *The Chalkboard*. If he does not guess correctly, the one who "signed" the dot becomes the new *Chalkboard*.

LOOK, SEE, LOOK

Equipment: None. The leader says to the players: "Look, see, look." The players reply: "What do we look for?" The leader says: "The letter 'M'" (or whatever may be the first letter of the object in the room that he is thinking about). Various players are questioned. The one who guesses correctly becomes the new leader.

NATURE STUDY

Equipment: None. A player chosen to be *It* stands in front of the class and describes a flower by size, shape, and color. The first player to guess the flower correctly, chases *It* to his seat. If he tags *It* before *It* can get to his seat, he becomes the new *It*. Descriptions of fish and birds may also be used.

NUMBER RACE

Equipment: Two sets of large cards numbered from 0–9. Two teams of ten players each line up facing one another across the room. Each player is given a card; a set goes to each team. When the leader calls out a number of two or more digits, the players from each team with those numbers walk out in front of their group in the proper order. The first team to do this scores a point. The leader then calls out another number combination. Addition and subtraction may also be employed.

PAPER PASSING

Equipment: A piece of newspaper for each row. The first player in each row is given a piece of newspaper crushed into the shape of a baton. He takes it in his left hand and hands it over his shoulder to the player seated directly behind him. This player receives it in his left hand and does the same thing. The process is repeated until the last player in the row has received the baton. He passes it back down the row with his right hand. The row that finishes first, wins the game.

PASS THE CLOTHESPINS

Equipment: Several clothespins or crayons for each team. Two teams line up facing each other across the room. When the leader says "Go," the first player on each team puts all his clothespins on the floor in front of the next player in his line. That player picks them up and places them in front of the next player. The first team to pass the clothespins all the way down its line is the winner.

PASS THE SHOE

Equipment: Various articles. The players are divided into teams lined up in single-file formations. In front of each line is a table. On each table are placed identical articles, such as chalkboard erasers, books, and rulers. When the signal to start is given, the first player on each team starts passing one of the articles down his line. Each player in the line must handle the article. When the article reaches the end of the line, it is started back again to the first player. Upon receiving the article, the first player places it on the table and starts the second article on its way. The first team to pass all of its articles down the line and back wins the game.

ROCK SCHOOL

Equipment: A small piece of chalk. Six lines, each representing a grade, are drawn on the floor. A player selected to be *The Teacher* stands at the head of the class. The other players, *The Class*, stand at the line representing the first grade. *The Teacher*, holding the piece of chalk in either hand with both fists clenched, stands in front of each player, in turn, and lets him guess which hand holds the piece of chalk. If a player guesses correctly, he goes on to the second grade. If he guesses correctly on his next turn, he advances to the third grade, etc. The first player to graduate from the sixth grade becomes the new *Teacher*.

SEVEN UP

Equipment: None. Seven players are chosen to be *Its*. The rest of the players must put their heads down. At the leader's signal, the *Its* walk around the room and tag one player each. Any player tagged must put his thumb up to denote to the other *Its* that he has been tagged. When all of the *Its* have tagged someone, they assemble at the front of the room and the leader says "Seven up." Those who have been tagged stand up. Each is permitted one guess as to who tagged him. If he guesses correctly, he changes places with the one who tagged him. If he does not guess correctly, he sits down. After all seven have guessed, the players standing at the front of the room go around and tag seven new players to be *Its*.

OUTDOOR GAMES

ADVANCING STATUES

Equipment: None. The players are lined up at a starting line. Each one demonstrates a pose that he will assume as a statue. An *It* is chosen and he stands about sixty feet away from the others with his back turned to them. It calls out "Start" and begins counting to ten. The other players advance as far as they can. When the count of ten is reached, *It* turns around. Anyone *It* sees moving or not in his demonstrated pose has to return to the starting line. Then *It* counts to ten again and the players advance once more. The first player to reach and touch *It* is the winner and becomes the new *It*.

ANIMAL CATCHER

Equipment: None. Two goal lines are designated about forty feet apart. In the middle of the playing area stands a player chosen to be *The Animal Catcher*. The other players stand on one of the goal lines facing *The Animal Catcher*. The leader gives them various animal names, such as *Horses, Tigers, Zebras, Lions,* etc. *The Animal Catcher* calls out the name of an animal—*Zebras*, for example—and all the *Zebras* skip (or walk fast) trying to get across to the other goal line without being tagged by *The Animal Catcher*. Those tagged have to help *The Animal Catcher* when he calls out the next group of animals.

BEANBAG BACKWARD RELAY

Equipment: Four beanbags. The players are divided into four equal teams facing in the same direction. At the leader's signal to go, the first player in each line drops a beanbag from behind his head to the ground. The second player in each line picks it up and does the same thing. This goes on until the last player in a line holds the beanbag over his head. The team finishing first scores one point. The last player in each line goes to the head of the line for the next game.

BROTHERS

Equipment: None. The players form two circles, one inside the other. The players in the outside circle face right and the players in the inside circle face left. When the signal to start is given, both circles start walking in the directions in which their players face. When the leader says "Stop," the players across from one another in the two circles join hands and stoop down. The last couple to stoop is out. The game continues until only one couple is left.

BULLETS

Equipment: A volleyball net and one utility ball. The players are divided into two teams, one team to each side of the net. The object of the game is to keep the ball on the other team's side of the net. Players must get rid of the ball as fast as possible. When the leader decides to call time, the team having possession of the ball gets a point against it. All returns must be over the net and within designated boundary lines.

CENTER BASE

Equipment: Playground ball. The players form a circle. A player chosen to stand in the center tosses the ball to any player in the circle and then runs outside the circle. The player to whom the ball is thrown must catch it, place it on the ground in the center of the circle, and try to tag the player who threw it. The player who threw the ball must try to get back to the center of the circle and touch the ball without getting tagged.

CHANGE PIN

Equipment: Two Indian clubs or plastic bottles. Two teams face each other about twenty yards apart. The players on each team count off so that there are corresponding numbers on each team. Two Indian clubs are placed on two circles drawn midway between the two teams and several yards apart. At the leader's signal, each Number One player runs out to his circle and picks up the Indian club from the edge of the circle and places it in the center of the circle. Then he tries to get back to his original position before his opponent can get back to his position. The winning runner is awarded one point. Then the leader calls out the next player. Each player runs to his circle and moves the Indian club from the center of the circle to the edge of the circle, its original place. The game goes on in this manner until everyone has had a turn. If an Indian Club falls down, the runner has to go back and stand it up again.

CIRCLE KICKBALL

Equipment: Playground ball. The players are arranged in a circle formation. A player in the circle is chosen to be *The Catcher*. The ball is started in play at the feet of the player to the right of *The Catcher*, who is called *The Kicker*. *The Kicker* kicks the ball across the circle and then runs around the outside of the circle. The other players recover the ball and pass it around the circle until it reaches *The Catcher*. If *The Kicker* returns to his place before *The Catcher* gets the ball, he scores a run. If he can make two trips around the circle before the ball reaches *The Catcher*, he scores two runs. If *The Catcher* gets the ball before *The Kicker* returns to his place, the player to the right of *The Kicker* becomes the next *Kicker*. The player scoring the most runs is the winner.

CIRCLE RELAY

Equipment: Two beanbags or paper towels. The players form two equal circles. The players in each circle are numbered consecutively. Number One holds a beanbag. At a signal from the leader, Number One in each circle runs around the outside of his circle and back to his original place. Then he hands his beanbag to the player on his right and the game continues. When a runner completes his turn, he kneels down. The first team whose players are all kneeling wins. Warn the players not to kneel with their feet in the way of the runners. Provide ample space between the circles to prevent runners from colliding.

CIRCLE STRIDE BALL

Equipment: Playground ball or soccer ball. The players stand in stride position in a circle formation; each foot touches the next player's foot. The ball is pushed around the circle in an attempt to make it go between one of the player's legs. If this happens, that player has a point scored against him. When a player has three points scored against him, he is eliminated. The ball can only be handled with the hands. Kneeling down or bending the knees is a violation of the rules; the offending player has a point scored against him. The last three players are declared the winners.

COME ALONG

Equipment: None. The players form a circle. Each player extends his left hand towards the middle of the circle. A player selected to be *It* walks around the inside of the circle and takes a player's hand. That player takes another player's hand, and so on, until seven players are walking around the circle in single file. Suddenly, *It* gives a signal and they all hurry back to their places. The last one back is *It* for the next game.

COMPLIANCE

Equipment: None. Two equal teams line up in single-file formations facing the leader. At the leader's command, everyone carries out an order. For instance, the leader may call out: "Get a leaf and hold it in your right hand. Go!" Then they line up at attention. The first team to comply wins. The players are to walk carefully when carrying out orders.

CORNER SPRY

Equipment: Four beanbags or balls. Four teams line up in four separate corners. The captain of each team stands in the center of the playing area. Each captain holds a beanbag and faces his team.

He throws the beanbag to each player on his team, and each player returns it to him. As the captain throws to his last player, he calls "Corner spry" and runs to the front of his team's line. Then, the last player in line becomes the new captain and the game goes on. The first team to have had all of its players be captains wins the game.

DEER RACE

Equipment: None. The players are divided into four groups. At a signal from the leader, the players in Group One run and touch a given object. The winner of the race goes to the side lines. Group Two then races, and the winner also goes to the side lines. After the four groups have raced, all the winners race to determine the fastest runner in *The Deer Herd*.

ERASER IN THE RING

Equipment: One chalkboard eraser and several beanbags. Draw a circle with a seven-foot diameter and place an eraser in its center. Space the players around the outside of the circle. A player selected to start the game slides a beanbag across the circle in an attempt to knock the eraser out of the circle. If successful, he scores a point. The game continues with the players on his right each taking a turn. The first player to score three points is the winner.

EXERCISE RELAY

Equipment: None. The players are arranged in two equal teams behind a designated line. At the leader's signal, the first player on each team runs to another line fifty feet away and performs an exercise. All the other players on his team must do the same exercise ten times in unison. Then the player returns to the end of his team. Each player who runs out to the line must do a different exercise for his team to follow. The first team to have all of its players back in their original positions wins.

FIRE ON THE MOUNTAIN

Equipment: None. The players form two circles, one inside the other, with everyone facing the center. A player is selected to stand in the center of the circles. The players chant: "Fire on the mountain, run boys run." As they chant, the outer circle runs to the right around the inner circle. While they are running, the player who stood in the middle joins them. When the leader calls "Stop," everyone in the outer circle tries to get a place behind one of the players in the inner circle. All players must go around the outside of the inner circle, running to their right, to get a place. The player who does not get a place becomes the player in the middle for the next game. The players in the inner circle then trade places with the players in the outer circle and the game goes on.

FIVE DOLLARS

Equipment: Softball and softball bat. The players are scattered over the field. One player bats the ball to the others. To catch a fly ball is worth one dollar, a ball caught on the first bounce is worth fifty cents, and a grounder is worth twenty-five cents. The object of the game is to see which player can get five dollars first. For variety, the player with the most money after a given length of time may trade places with the batter.

GIANT'S CAVE

Equipment: None. The players line up side by side facing in the same direction. One player is chosen to be *The Giant* and another to be *The Mother.* When *The Mother* calls "Here comes *The Giant,*" all the other players try to get to a section designated as *Home.* *The Giant* tries to tag as many as possible. Everyone that he catches has to stand in *The Giant's Cave.* After *The Giant* has had three turns, he announces: "I have caught .... children. I now choose ...... to be the new *Giant.*" *The Giant* also selects a new *Mother.*

HOP ALONG

Equipment: None. The players are arranged in a large circle. An *It* is chosen to hop around the outside of the circle. *It* stops behind five different players, saying "Hop along" each time. They hop after him. Suddenly, *It* calls "Run home," and they all try to get a place in the circle. The player who fails to get a place becomes *It.*

HOT POTATO

Equipment: Beanbag or playground ball. The players stand in a circle and pass the beanbag from one to another. Throwing is not allowed. A leader stands in the middle of the circle with his eyes closed. When he calls out "Halt," the player holding the beanbag is eliminated from the game.

JUMP THE SHOT

Equipment: A rope with a towel tied to one end. The players stand facing in a circle. A player selected to be *The Twirler* stands in the middle of the circle and swings the rope around at foot level. The players in the circle try to jump the rope when it reaches their feet. If a player stops the rope three times, he is eliminated. Observe *The Twirler* for signs of dizziness. Insist that the rope be swung low to avoid injuries.

KEEP AWAY TOUCH BALL

Equipment: Utility ball. The players are arranged in a circle formation, and an *It* is chosen to stand inside the circle. A ball is passed from player to player around and across the circle. *It* tries to tag the ball. If he does, the player who handled it last becomes *It*.

KICKBALL

Equipment: Soccer ball or playground ball, a softball diamond or bases. This game is played exactly like softball, except that the ball is kicked rather than batted. The ball is rolled to the kicker by the pitcher. No bunting is allowed.

LAST COUPLE OUT

Equipment: None. The players line up as couples behind a player chosen to be *It*. When *It* claps his hands and says "Last couple out," the last couple in line separates. The person on the right runs to the right, and the one on the left runs to the left. They try to join hands again before *It* can tag either of them. The one tagged first becomes the new *It*. The new couple then takes a place at the head of the line behind *It* and the game goes on. If *It* fails to tag either one, he has to call out the next couple.

LAST ONE TO TAG

Equipment: None. The players are divided into two teams. One team stands on one half of a circle or square and the other team stands on the other half. A player from each team goes to the center; one of them is chosen to be *It*. At a signal from the leader, *It* tries to tag his opponent. If he tags him, his opponent tries to tag him back. When the leader calls "Stop," a point is scored by the player who is not *It*. Players must stay within the circle.

LEADER BALL

Equipment: Two utility balls. The players are formed into teams of two circles. Each team has a ball. At a signal from the leader, the captain of each team passes the ball to the player on his right. This player passes the ball to the player on his right. This continues until the ball makes a complete circuit and is returned to the captain. When the captain receives the ball he calls out "One" and passes the ball on for circuit number two, etc. The first team to complete five circuits is the winner.

LINE BALL

Equipment: Two softball bats and one softball. Two teams line up behind opposite goal lines, seventy feet apart. Each team has a bat, but both teams use the same ball. A player at one end of one of the teams starts the game by tossing the ball up and trying to bat it across the opponents' goal line. If successful, he scores a point for his team. To count as a score, the ball must be batted on the ground, or at least below shoulder level. The teams take turns batting. Play continues until every player has had a chance to bat. Each player is permitted only one swing. The team with the most points scored is the winner. Warn the players to remain a safe distance from the player who is batting the ball.

LINE SOCCER

Equipment: Soccer ball or playground ball. Two teams face one another on goal lines about twenty yards apart. To start the game, a player from each team comes to the center of the playing area and puts his right foot on the ball. At a signal from the leader, each of these players attempts to kick the ball across the other team's goal line. The players on the goal lines are only permitted to kick the ball back out to their center players. A point is scored when the ball crosses the opponent's goal line below shoulder level; a ball kicked higher does not count as a score. After every goal, or when the leader calls time, new center players come from the goal lines. Players can use their hands only to protect their faces from a kicked ball.

ONE OLD CAT

Equipment: A softball and a softball bat; a softball diamond or two bases. In this softball game, the batter stays at bat until he makes an out. Each time the batter hits the ball he tries to run to first and back without being put out. Each time he is successful, he scores a point. When a batter is out, he goes to right field. Then the right fielder goes to center field, the center fielder moves to left field, the left fielder goes to third base, etc. Outs are made when the ball is caught on the fly or is thrown to first base or home before the batter reaches first or home.

OVER AND UNDER RELAY

Equipment: Four playground balls. The players form four teams lined up in single-file formations. The first player on each team has a ball. At a signal from the leader, he passes it over his head to the player behind him. This player then passes the ball between his legs to the next player. The game continues in this manner, the ball going down the line over the head of one player and between the legs of the next. When the ball reaches the end of the line, the last player in the line runs with it to the head of the line. The team that is the first to return the ball to its original position is the winner.

PASS AND STOOP BASKETBALL

Equipment: Two junior-size basketballs; a basketball court. The players are divided into two teams. Each team has a basketball and scatters over its own half of a basketball court. At a signal from the leader, the player with the ball throws a chest pass to another player and then stoops down. The player receiving the pass passes off to another player and then he stoops down, too. The game continues this way until the last player standing on one team scores a basket before the last player standing on the other team can. A point is scored by the first player to shoot a basket. The player scoring the basket starts the next game.

POISON HOLDER

Equipment: Any object. The players scatter over a playing area designated by the leader. An *It* is selected to start out with the object (*Poison Holder*). He chases the other players until he tags one. Then that person is the new *It* and has to take the object. No player may refuse to accept the *Poison Holder*.

REACHING FIRST

Equipment: A softball and a softball bat; a softball diamond or two bases. This game is the same as regular softball, except that no base running is permitted beyond first base and the entire team bats in each inning. When a batter is either safe at first base or out, he withdraws and the next batter takes his turn. One point is scored for each player reaching first safely. Teams change places only after every player has had a turn at bat. Any number of innings may be played.

RESCUE RELAY

Equipment: None. The players are divided into two teams. Each team lines up in single file behind a selected leader. A *Rescuer* is stationed fifty feet away from each team. At a signal, *The Rescuers* run forward, take the hands of the first players on each team, and run back to their original places. The players rescued become *Rescuers*. The game continues until all the players have been brought over and are standing in new lines. The first team to complete its new line is the winner.

RUN AND ROLL BACK RELAY

Equipment: Four playground balls. Divide the players into four teams standing in single-file formations. At a given signal, the first player on each team runs to a designated line and rolls a ball back to the next player on his team. The player receiving the ball repeats the process, and so on. The team that gets all of its players across the finish line first is the winner.

SARDINES

Equipment: None. A player is chosen to be *The Sardine.* While the other players close their eyes, he hunts for a hiding place. When the leader gives the signal, the rest of the players look for *The Sardine.* When a player finds *The Sardine,* he tries to hide with him. The hunting continues until all the players are packed into *The Sardine's* hiding place. The first player to discover *The Sardine* becomes *The Sardine* for the next game.

SEATTLE

Equipment: None. The players are divided into two teams, Team A and Team B. The two teams stand at opposite ends of the playing area. The players on Team A get together and decide on actions they will imitate, such as riding a bike or bouncing a ball. After deciding what they will do, they walk up to Team B and their leader calls on various players on Team B to try to guess what the action represents. When someone on Team B guesses correctly, all the players on Team A run back to their home side while the Team B players try to tag as many of them as possible. All those tagged become members of Team B. Then the teams exchange roles.

SIX PASSES

Equipment: Two junior-size basketballs; a basketball court. Two circles of players are formed, one at each end of a basketball court. Each circle numbers off. At a signal from the leader, each Number One has to complete six passes to six different players in his circle. Then he must dribble in to his team's basket and try to make a goal before his opponent can do the same thing at the other end. The winner scores one point for his team. The game goes on with the two Number Two players, and so on.

SNOW WHITE

Equipment: None. A girl is chosen to be *Snow White;* she lives in *The Castle.* Another player is selected to be *The Witch;* she lives in

The Dungeon. The rest of the players are *Dwarfs* and are divided
into one of these groups: *Grumpy, Dopey, Sleepy, Happy, Bashful,
Doc, and Sneezy. The Witch* calls out the name of one of the groups
of *Dwarfs.* All who have that name run to an area called *The
Mountain* and then return home. *The Witch* tries to tag as many
as she can. All those tagged must go to *The Dungeon.* Then *The
Witch* calls another group. The only way a *Dwarf* can be rescued
is for *Snow White* to touch his outstretched hand in *The Dungeon.*
If she touches one, he may walk back to *Snow White's Castle* and
then to his home. If *Snow White* is tagged by *The Witch,* she must
return to *The Castle* till the next group is called. Two *Witches* may
be used. One rests while the other is trying to catch *Dwarfs* and
guard *The Dungeon. The Witch* who is resting is not permitted to
tag anyone.

SOCCER GOLF

Equipment: Two soccer balls and two large boxes or wastebaskets.
Two teams form single-file formations facing in the same direction
behind a restraining line. A cardboard box is placed on its side
forty yards in front of each team. At a signal, the first player on
each team kicks a ball until it rolls into the box. The player who
makes it in the least number of kicks wins a point for his team.
This game can be used as a relay race, with each player kicking the
ball into the box, removing it, and kicking it back to the next
player in line, who repeats the process. The team finishing first
wins. Use of the hands is permitted only when the player removes
the ball from the box for his return trip.

SOCCER KICK FOR DISTANCE

Equipment: Two soccer balls. Two teams stand facing in the same
direction in single-file formations behind a restraining line. At a
signal, the first player on each team kicks a ball along the ground.
The one whose ball rolls the farthest is the winner and scores a
point for his team. The two kickers then go to the end of their lines
and the next players in line kick. The game continues until everyone
has had a chance to kick. The team that scores the most points
is the winner.

SOFTBALL BOUNCE

Equipment: A softball and a softball bat; a softball diamond. Players station themselves as in softball. The pitcher must toss the softball easy to give the batter a good chance to hit it. A ball caught on the fly or on the first bounce allows the player catching it to become the new batter. No running is involved in this game. Rotate the pitcher and the catcher at frequent intervals.

SPUD

Equipment: Small playground ball. The players form a circle. A player chosen to start the game stands in the middle and tosses the ball up in the air. As he does this, he calls out the name of a player in the circle. This player must retrieve the ball and yell "Spud." When the other players hear this they must freeze at once. The player catching the ball then throws at any nearby player and tries to hit him below the waist. That player tries to dodge, but he may move only one foot. If he gets hit by the ball, an "S" is scored against his name. If the thrower misses, an "S" is scored against his name. The second time a player has a point against him, the letter "P" is added; the third time, it is "U." When the word "Spud" is completed, he is out of the game. The player who gets a point against his name tosses the next ball in the air.

SQUIRREL IN THE CAGE

Equipment: None. Groups of threes scatter over the playing area. Two players of each group act as *The Cage.* The third player is *The Squirrel* and stands between the other two. Several extra *Squirrels* are added to the middle of the playing area. At the leader's signal, all *Squirrels* change cages and the extra *Squirrels* seek cages. After several exchanges, have *The Squirrels* change places with some of the players who are *The Cages.* Have other exchanges later until every player has had a chance to be a *Squirrel.*

STEAL THE BACON

Equipment: A towel or some other soft object. The players are divided into two equal teams that face each other lined up behind designated lines. A towel is placed midway between the two teams.

Players on the teams are given corresponding numbers. When a number is called, the player on each team with that number goes out and tries to grab the towel and return to his position without being tagged by the other player. If a player takes the towel and returns without being tagged, he scores a point for his team. If the other player tags him, that player scores a point for his team.

TARGET BALL

Equipment: A utility ball and an Indian club or plastic bottle. Two equal teams stand in single-file formations facing each other about thirty feet apart. Between the two teams is an Indian club. The players, in turn, try to bowl down the club. If a player misses the pin he goes to the end of his line and waits for his next turn. The teams alternate in bowling at the pin.

THREE DEEP

Equipment: None. The players form two circles, one inside the other. Each player in the outer circle stands directly behind a player in the inner circle. Two players are chosen to go outside the circle. One is *The Runner;* the other is *The Chaser.* Starting out on opposite sides of the outer circle, *The Chaser* tries to tag *The Runner. The Runner* can save himself by standing between a player in the outer circle and a player in the inner circle. Then the player in the outer circle becomes *The Runner.* The new *Runner* can save himself by getting between another couple. All running must be done on the outside of the outer circle, except when *The Runner* wants to save himself.

THROW AWAY

Equipment: Two playground balls. The players are divided into two teams standing in single-file formations. At a signal from the leader, the first player on each team throws his team's ball as far as he can and then runs after the ball thrown by his opponent. The first player to retrieve a ball and come back to the head of his line scores a point for his team. After completing his turn, a player goes to the end of his line and the game goes on. This game can also be used as a relay.

WASHINGTON SOFTBALL

Equipment: A softball and a softball bat; a softball diamond. This game is the same as softball, except that whenever a batter hits a fair ball he must run the bases until he scores a run or is put out. He scores a point for each base reached. In other words, if a player hits the ball and arrives safely at first base, he must continue towards second; but even if he is put out at second, he scores one point. A home run scores four points. After three outs, the teams change positions. Any number of innings may be played.

GRADES 5-6

INDOOR GAMES

ALL WORDS

Equipment: Paper and pencils or chalk and chalkboard. The players
are told to write all the words they can think of that begin with
one letter ("s," for example) and end with another letter ("m,"
for example, to form "steam, scream, stream," etc.). A point is
scored for each correct word.

AROUND THE ROOM

Equipment: Two chalkboard erasers or two beanbags. A boy and a
girl are selected to come to the front of the room. The leader stands
there with an eraser in each hand. At a signal from the leader, each
player takes an eraser from the leader's outstretched hands, walks
around the room, and places the eraser in the leader's other hand.

The first player to complete the circuit wins. One point is scored for each win, and the team (boys versus girls) with the most points wins. Hopping, skipping, etc., may be used; but make sure that there are no obstacles to cause accidents.

ASSOCIATION

Equipment: A pencil and cards or a chalkboard and chalk. On separate cards, write two words that go together, such as "bread" and "butter," "ham" and "eggs," etc. When the leader flashes a card, the first player to call the related word wins that card. The player who collects the most cards is the winner. You could also have players go to the chalkboard and write the word corresponding to the one called out. Cities and states or states and capitals may also be used.

BOWLING RELAY

Equipment: A small playground ball for each team. Chairs are arranged so that they form bowling alleys. Each row of players makes up a team. Each team selects a captain to stand at one end of its row. At a signal, each captain rolls a ball to the first player on his team. That player rolls the ball back to him and sits down in his seat. This goes on until the captain receives the ball back from the last player in line. Then he holds the ball over his head to signify that his team has finished. A point is scored for each win. New captains are chosen after every game.

CHALKBOARD RELAY

Equipment: Chalkboard and chalk. Instead of touching a goal in this relay race, each player writes a number on the chalkboard. The last player on each team must add all the numbers that the other players on his team have written on the chalkboard. The winner is the team that finishes first with its numbers added correctly.

DROP BEANBAG RELAY

Equipment: A beanbag for each row. The players are lined up in single file in equal teams. All are standing. The first player on each team is given a beanbag. At the word "Go," he raises the beanbag over his head and drops it behind him. The next player in line bends over and picks up the beanbag and repeats the process. When the last player in the row picks up the beanbag, he holds it up in the air to signify that his row has finished. The team finishing first is the winner. For variety, the players may change places for each game.

ERASER BALANCE

Equipment: A chalkboard eraser for each row. The players are divided into equal rows. All are seated. The players in the rows number off consecutively at the same time, so that each row is identical. The leader then calls a number. The player with that number from each row walks briskly to an eraser placed in front of his row, picks it up and passes it around his waist three times, stands it on its end, and tries to get back to his place before the others return to their places. The winner of each race scores a point for his row.

GEOGRAPHY

Equipment: None. The players stand or sit in a line. The first player names a geographical location. The next player in line names a place that begins with the last letter of the previously named word. The only requirement is that the cities, rivers, lakes, etc., must be on the map. For example, the first player may say "Idaho"; the second, "Oregon"; and the third, "Nevada." A player unable to name a place within a specified period of time is eliminated. The player who stays in the game the longest is the winner.

THE MOON IS ROUND

Equipment: A piece of chalk. The players sit in a circle. The leader draws a face with his left hand, saying: "The moon is round. It has two eyes, a nose, a mouth, and two ears." The leader then asks if anyone can do exactly what he has just done. The volunteer must imitate what the leader says and does exactly. The trick is that the average player, unless he is left-handed, will pick up the chalk with his right hand and draw the face. Variations can include a slight cough to clear the throat, etc.

OBSERVATION

Equipment: Ten to twelve objects of any description, a sheet of paper or cloth, and paper and pencils. The objects are placed on a table. The players walk by the table, look at the objects, and return to their seats. The objects are then covered and the players take paper and pencil and write down the names of as many items as they can recall seeing. The player who lists the greatest number of items correctly wins the game.

OLD SAYINGS

Equipment: Paper and pencil. Write down familiar sayings on slips of paper and then cut them in two. Distribute the tabs to the players. The players must find the person with the other half of their saying. For instance, "cold as ice" is written down and divided after "cold as." The player who has the slip of paper with "cold as" written on it must find the person with the slip saying "ice." The first couple to complete a saying wins.

SALESMAN

Equipment: Ten articles. A player is chosen to be *The Salesman.* He must sell ten articles to ten different players. When a buyer makes a purchase, he puts it out of sight. When *The Salesman* has sold all his articles, he must remember what he sold and to whom he sold it. He then tries to buy the articles back. The leader keeps track of the sales and keeps score on how many correct buys *The Salesman* makes.

SCOUTING FOR WORDS

Equipment: None. A word is written on the chalkboard. The letters appearing in the word are to be rearranged to make other words. The player who compiles the longest list of words from the original word is the winner.

SENTENCE RELAY

Equipment: Chalkboard and chalk. The players are seated in equal rows. The chalkboard is divided into as many sections as there are rows. A piece of chalk is placed in front of each row. At a signal, the first player in each row walks to the chalkboard, writes a word to begin a sentence, and returns to his seat. The second player then goes to the chalkboard and adds a word to the sentence started by the first player. The first team to compose a complete sentence in which each player has written a word wins the game.

SIDEWARD PASS RELAY

Equipment: A chalkboard eraser for each team. Each row has an equal number of players. Those in the first seats of each row make up a team, those in the second seats make up a team, etc. Each player on one of the outside rows is given an eraser. At the leader's command, he hands his eraser to the next player. The team that completes the relay first is the winner.

TWENTY QUESTIONS

Equipment: Paper and pencils. Each player writes the name of a person, place, or thing on a piece of paper. When it is his turn, he tells the group if the thing he has named is animal, vegetable, or mineral. The other players may ask a total of twenty questions to find out the subject. The questions must be the kind that can be answered by a yes or no. The first person to guess correctly may then ask the players to identify his subject. If a subject is not guessed in twenty questions, the player gives the correct answer and selects another player to take his place.

WHO AM I?

Equipment: None. A player is selected to represent any famous person in history that he chooses. The other players ask him questions that can be answered with a yes or no. After ten players guess incorrectly, the player tells the group his identity and chooses a new personality. If a questioner guesses correctly, he represents a famous person of his own choosing. Leading questions, such as "Are you living?" and "Were you a general?", should be encouraged. For variation, sports figures and entertainment personalities may be used.

OUTDOOR GAMES

AROUND THE WORLD

Equipment: Junior-size basketball; a basketball court. Consecutive numbers are drawn on the court at intervals in front of a basket. Starting with the lowest number, each player, in turn, tries to shoot a basket from each numbered spot. He must make a basket before he can move to the next position. If he misses, he must wait for his next turn and try to make the basket again. The first player to make a basket from each position is the winner. An alternate plan is to let each player shoot until he makes a basket from each position. The one with the lowest number of shots is the winner.

BASE TOUCH RELAY

Equipment: Softball; a softball diamond or four bases. The players are divided into two teams, the running team and the fielding team. The object of the game is for the runner to beat the ball around the bases. The fielding team has players stationed at first, second, third, and home plate. Both the ball and the runner start from home plate when the leader says "Go." Each baseman receiving the ball must tag his base before he throws it on to the next baseman. If the runner reaches home plate before the ball, he scores a point for his team. Basemen should be rotated frequently by the fielding team to provide greater participation. After each player on the running team has had a turn, the fielding team has its opportunity to score points.

BASKETBALL DRIBBLE RELAY

Equipment: Two junior-size basketballs; a basketball court. Two teams line up in single-file formations at one end of the basketball court facing the opposite basket. At a signal from the leader, the first player on each team dribbles down the court and takes one shot at the basket and, whether he makes it or not, dribbles back and places the ball on the floor in front of the next player on his team. This player then picks up the ball and repeats the procedure. The game goes on until every player has had a turn. Each basket counts as two points. The team finishing the race first is granted a bonus of two points to add to their total. The team with the higher score wins.

BATTING TEE DRILL

Equipment: A softball bat, a softball, and a batting tee; a softball diamond. The players space themselves around the infield of a softball diamond from first to third base. A player starts the activity by batting the softball from the tee. Each player takes a turn batting from the tee and then lays the bat on the ground for the next player. After each turn, the players move clockwise one position. The player nearest the batted ball retrieves it and rolls it in to the next batter. No players are permitted near the person batting.

BOMBARDMENT

Equipment: Eight Indian clubs or plastic bottles and four playground balls. Two equal teams face each other across a playing area divided by a center line. Each team spaces four Indian clubs on a goal line fifty feet away from the center dividing line. A guard is chosen by each team to protect its clubs, and he is the only player allowed near them. The other players stand behind their goal lines and throw the balls at their opponent's clubs. Each club knocked down counts as a point for the throwing team. If a guard accidentally knocks over a club, it counts as a point for his opponents. A guard is not permitted to throw at his opponents' clubs.

BOMBERS ATTACK

Equipment: Six playground balls. Two equal teams are stationed at opposite ends of a playing area divided by a center line. Each team is given three playground balls. At a signal from the leader, all the players approach the center line and start throwing the balls at their opponents. Any player hit below the waist is eliminated and goes to the side lines. The team that has the most players remaining when time is called is the winner.

BOUNCE AND PASS RELAY

Equipment: Four playground balls. Four teams stand in single-file formations, with an arm's length space between each player on a team. At the leader's signal, the first player on each team bounces his ball on the ground and hands it back over his head to the next player in line, who continues the activity. When the last player in line receives the ball, he runs to the front of the line and bounces the ball and hands it back. This continues until all players are back to their original positions in line. The team that finishes first is the winner.

BOUNDARY BALL

Equipment: Playground ball. Two teams stand in their own halves of a playing area about the size of a basketball court with a clearly marked dividing line in its center. Players score a point for their team by throwing the ball across the other team's goal line. Players may block their opponent's throws from going across their goal line. After each point, the ball is put in play from the center by the team that lost the point. The team that scores the most points is the winner.

CATCH TEN

Equipment: Three playground balls. Three teams are arranged in circle formations. At the leader's signal, each team tries to pass its ball around its circle ten times without letting it touch the ground. Each time the ball makes a circuit around the circle, the number of the circuit is called out. The first team to make ten circuits with the ball is the winner.

CATCH THE FLY

Equipment: A junior-size football for each group. The players are divided into small groups. A player in each group kicks a ball. Any player in his group who catches the ball on the fly changes places with the kicker. If no one catches the ball on the fly after three kicks, the kicker chooses his own replacement. Girls may play this game with a soccer ball or playground ball.

COUGAR

Equipment: None. A player is selected to be the *Cougar.* The other players venture near *The Cougar's Den* and taunt him by calling: "*Cougar, Cougar,* come out of your *Den,* the player you catch will be one of your men." At this, *The Cougar* tries to catch as many players as possible by touching them and saying "Cougar." All those caught become *Cougars* and assist *The Cougar.*

FOOTBALL GOLF

Equipment: Two junior-size footballs and two wastebaskets or cardboard boxes. Two teams line up in single-file formations. Fifty yards in front of each team, a wastebasket is placed on its side with its top facing the team. The object of the game is for a kicker to punt the ball as near to the wastebasket as possible and then kick it into the wastebasket with the side of his foot. After doing this, he retrieves the ball from the basket and runs back and hands it to the next runner in line, who repeats the process. The team finishing first wins. Girls may play this game with a kickball.

GOAL SHOOTING BASKETBALL

Equipment: A basketball for each team; a basketball court. Two teams line up in single-file formations in front of the basket. At the leader's signal, the first player on each team dribbles to the basket and shoots until he makes a basket. After making a basket, a player must dribble back to his team and hand the ball to the next player in line. The game goes on till every player has had a turn. The team whose players all score a basket before its opponents all score a basket wins.

GUARD THE CASTLE

Equipment: A milk carton or plastic bottle and a utility ball. A circle is formed and a player is selected to go into the middle to protect *The Castle* (milk carton). He is not permitted to use his hands. The players in the circle kick the ball trying to knock down *The Castle*. When a player knocks over the castle, he changes places with the guard.

JUMP ROPE RELAY

Equipment: Four jump ropes. Four teams stand in single-file formations about forty feet behind a designated goal line. At a signal from the leader, the first player on each team picks up his rope and skips rope to the goal line and back. The next player in line takes the rope and repeats the process. The team finishing first is the winner.

KANGAROO RELAY

Equipment: Four playground balls. Four teams line up in single-file formations forty feet behind a goal line. The first player in each line places a ball between his knees and hops to the goal line and back again. Then he hands the ball to the next player in line, who repeats the process. The game goes on until one team completes the race. If a player drops the ball, he must pick it up and start again from the place he dropped it. A player may not use his hands to keep the ball from falling from between his knees.

MISS PIN

Equipment: A playground ball and three Indian clubs for each team. The players are divided into two or three teams. Three clubs are spaced out two feet apart before each team. The teams stand in single-file formations. The object of this game is to try to miss the clubs. Every club knocked down counts as a point against the team bowling. Every player bowls once, in turn. At the end of the game, each team adds up its score. The team with the lowest score is the winner.

NO BAT SOFTBALL

Equipment: Softball; a softball diamond. This game is played like softball, except that the "batter" catches the ball from the pitcher and throws it. This is a good activity to improve throwing, fielding, and base-running skills.

NUMBER BASKETBALL

Equipment: Two junior-size basketballs and two towels; a basketball court. Two teams are given identical sets of consecutive numbers. When the leader calls out a number, the players with that number on each team run out to the center of the court. There, two basketballs previously assigned to the teams rest on towels to keep them stationary. Each player picks up his ball and dribbles to either basket and tries to make a basket before his opponent does. Play is terminated when either of the players scores. Each basket counts two points if scored before the opponent scores. If both players score at the same time, it is called a tie and each team is awarded two points.

OBJECT RELAY

Equipment: Four jump ropes, four softballs, and four playground balls. The players line up single file in four equal teams. In front of each team place a jump rope, a softball, and a playground ball, with about five yards between each object. At a signal from the leader, the first player on each team runs to the jump rope and jumps ten times. Then he drops the rope and runs to the softball, picks it up, and tosses it in the air ten times. Then he runs to the playground ball, bounces it ten times, and returns and tags the next runner in his line, who repeats the process. The team that completes the race first is the winner.

OBSTACLE RELAY

Equipment: None. Two teams sit in rows on the ground, with the players' feet stretched out in the same direction. At a signal from the leader, the first player on each team stands and starts running and leaping over the outstretched feet of the rest of the players in his line. After hurdling the last player's feet, he runs behind his own line back to his place and sits down. The second runner then repeats the process, including jumping over the first runner's feet before he takes his original place in line. The race continues until all have had a chance to run and a winner is decided upon. Warn the players to keep their feet straight and the runners to be careful as they jump over them.

PARTNER SNATCH

Equipment: None. The players stand in couples to form a double circle formation. One circle faces right and the other circle faces left. At a signal from the leader, each circle of players walks in the direction it is facing. When the leader calls "Stop," they try to locate their partners and then stoop. The last couple to stoop is eliminated from the game. The players may not cut through the circle to find their partners.

PASS AND CATCH RELAY

Equipment: Two playground balls. The players are divided into two teams. They choose partners and stand in columns of twos facing in the same direction. A goal line is designated twenty-five yards away. At a signal from the leader, the first two players on each team run to the goal line and back again. As they run, they pass a ball back and forth between them. The next two players in line repeat the process, and the game goes on until one of the teams finishes.

PIN FOOTBALL

Equipment: Two Indian clubs and one junior-size football; a softball diamond. The players are divided into two teams, a kicking team and a fielding team. Indian clubs are placed on first base and home plate. The fielding team scatters over the playing area, with one player standing at first base and another at home plate (the only two bases used). A kicker punts the football, runs around the first base club, and tries to get back to the home plate club before the fielding team can: (1) recover the ball, (2) throw it to the first base player, who (3) knocks down his club and (4) throws the ball to the catcher, who (5) knocks down the club at home plate. One point is scored for each run. After three outs, the teams trade places. A punt caught on the fly is an out. Rotate the first base and catching positions to give more players the opportunity to handle the ball.

PIN SOCCER

Equipment: One soccer ball and two Indian clubs or plastic bottles. Two teams face each other about ninety feet apart. Restraining lines are drawn before each team. The members of each team stand side-by-side an arm's length apart. Ten feet in front of each team is an Indian club. Two players from each team come out to the center of the playing area. Each places his right foot on the ball. At a signal from the leader, they start kicking the ball in an attempt to knock over their opponent's club. If neither club has been knocked over after a minute, time is called and two more players come out and have a try at it. The players behind the restraining lines may only kick the ball back to their players in the center. Only the players in the center may score points. One point is scored each time a club is knocked over.

POTATO RACE

Equipment: Four wooden blocks or chalkboard erasers for each team. Four teams line up in single-file formations behind a designated starting line. In front of each squad are lined up four circles spaced ten feet apart. A wooden block is inside each circle. At the leader's signal, the first player in each line runs to the first circle and picks up the block. Then he returns it to the starting line and runs out and picks up the second block, etc., until all the blocks are at the starting line. The next runner on each team must replace the blocks one at a time. The team completing the race first wins.

PUNT BACK

Equipment: Junior-size football. Two teams stand facing each other on goal lines sixty yards apart. The players try to punt the ball across the field and over the other team's goal line on the fly without being caught by an opponent. Every ball kicked over an opponent's goal line on the fly without being caught counts as one point. The team scoring the point must then start play by kicking the ball from their own goal line. A kick touched by a player before it goes over the goal line must be kicked again from the point of contact. If a player catches a kick on the fly behind his own goal line, he comes out to his own goal line and kicks the ball.

SOCCER DODGE BALL

Equipment: Soccer ball. Two teams are selected. One team forms a large circle and the other team scatters inside the circle. The team on the circle tries to eliminate the players inside by hitting them with the kicked soccer ball. After three minutes, the teams change positions and the game goes on. The team that has the most players remaining in the circle is the winner. Use of the hands is not permitted.

SOCCER DRIBBLE RELAY

Equipment: A soccer ball and an Indian club or plastic bottle for each team. Four teams line up in single-file formations behind a restraining line. An Indian club is placed fifty feet in front of each team. At the leader's signal, the first player in each line kicks his ball out to and around his team's marker and back to the feet of the next player on his team. The game goes on till all the players on one team have finished. Players may use their feet only. Any club knocked down, either by the ball or the kicker's foot, must be set up at once by the kicker.

SOFTBALL THROW FOR ACCURACY

Equipment: A softball and an Indian club or plastic bottle for each team. Teams are lined up in single-file formations. At the leader's signal, the first player in each line throws at an Indian club placed about fifty feet in front of his team. A player scores a point for his team each time he knocks over a club. The throwers throw on command from the leader. Then they go out and retrieve the softballs they threw and hand them to the next players on their teams. The game goes on until every player has had a turn.

TAG BASE RELAY

Equipment: Softball; a softball diamond. Players are assigned to first base, second base, third base and home plate. A fifth player is chosen to be the runner. At the leader's signal, the runner starts from home plate and tries to tag all the bases, in order, before each baseman can catch the ball and tag his base. If a runner reaches home plate before the ball, he scores a point. Players are rotated until all have had a chance to be the runner. Then five more players are chosen to play.

TWENTY-ONE BASKETBALL

Equipment: Basketball; a basketball court. The players line up in front of the basket. Each player shoots one long shot and one short shot when it is his turn. If a player misses with his long shot, he does not get to try for a short shot. A long shot counts as two points; a short shot (lay up) counts one point. The first player to score twenty-one points wins.

WHIRLAWAY

Equipment: None. Two equal teams stand facing each other across a fifty-foot space. The players on both teams are given corresponding numbers. When the leader calls out a number, the players from both teams with that number come out to the center of the playing area, join both hands, and start twirling around in a clockwise direction. When the leader says "Whirlaway," they drop their hands and try to return to their places. One point is scored each time a player gets back to his team before his opponent. The team with the most points at the end of the game is the winner.

WOOD TAG

Equipment: None. All the players except one chosen to be *It* scatter over the playing area. *It* tries to tag the other players. A player is safe as long as he is touching wood of some sort. A player not touching wood may be tagged by *It*. If he is tagged, he becomes the *It* for the next game.

ZIG-ZAG SOCCER RELAY

Equipment: A soccer ball and four Indian clubs for each team. Four teams line up in single-file formations facing Indian clubs placed several feet apart in front of them. At a signal from the leader, the first player in each line dribbles his ball with his feet in and out between the clubs and back to the next player on his team, who repeats the process. The game goes on until every player has had a turn. The team whose last player completes the race first wins. In case of a tie, the team that has knocked over the least clubs wins the game.

INDEX